Mar 15. 2019

To: Megan
With Love,
Gloria

P.S. This book was written by
a family friend & former
member of Shandon —

MW00565506

WHISPERS FROM GOD

A 30-Day Devotional

MELLIE BOOZER

Cover painting: Carol Parente
Photographed by: Katie Hilliger
Cover design: Jerry Axson

ISBN: 978-1-54395-452-4

TABLE OF CONTENTS

INTRODUCTION

'God, are you speaking or are these just my own thoughts? How am I supposed to know?!' Have you been there, too? For the longest time I struggled with the mystery of how to hear God's voice. I'd listen to people talk about what God had told them and wonder if He'd ever speak to me like that. 'God, why can't I hear you? Is it me? What am I doing wrong?' It took some time, prayer, and many conversations with people who hear God clearly, but one day I had a revelation.

I had been waiting to hear some loud audible voice thundering down from the heavens, but that's not always how God speaks. Many times God whispers. He whispers to us through His scripture, through nature, and through songs. He speaks through other people in sermons, books, and conversations, and He gives us that "gut feeling" (also known as the Holy Spirit) to let us know what He's saying. We can be assured that it's God speaking if it lines up with the truth of the Bible and if we have a deep-seated peace about it.

I also realized I have to take the time to actually be still and *listen*. Wow, what a concept, right? I quickly figured out that I had been the one doing all of the talking during my times with God. Oops! In the span of a few days, two different people in my life who don't even know each other, challenged me to start taking time to get quiet before God and to write down anything I heard Him whispering to me. Once I got quiet enough to listen, it was amazing! He spoke of His love, He reminded me of His truths, and He encouraged me with His promises. No matter what I was going through, He whispered just what I needed to hear.

I wrote everything down and several months later, He told me to share with you all that He'd spoken to me. I knew the idea of writing a devotional book was from Him because it's not something I've ever even thought of doing. I was the one always telling others that they were amazing writers and should write a book. Well, the joke's on me because here we are! Trust me, God loves to speak to His children and you can absolutely hear Him when you take the time to listen.

HERE WE GO!

This book includes 30 days of devotionals written to encourage you with what I believe God wants you to know. He spoke these very words to me to share with you. May they bless your entire life.

Take time to read, pray, declare, and meditate over the accompanying scriptures. Speak them out loud, remembering this is God's living and active Word, which has undeniable power.

Now it's your turn to be still and listen. Find a quiet place that works for you (at home, out in nature, etc.,) and ask God, "What would you like to say to me today? What would you like me to know?" He may whisper to you regarding a specific situation you're going through or He may remind you exactly how He feels about you. He may use some of the scripture you just read to continue to speak His truth.

There is space to write down what He whispers in your ear. It's amazing to be able to look back over time and be reminded of what He's said concerning you.

My prayer is that you would continue to make time to hear the sweet voice of God and that you'll go on to encourage others with His words. I can't wait to hear some of the things God shares with you! Now, listen closely...

DAY 1
A NEW ADVENTURE

My child, join me on a new adventure. I'm strategically putting all of the pieces of your life together so the masterfully completed puzzle can be revealed in due time. It may not make sense to you now, but you'll be amazed when my perfect plans unfold before your very eyes. Take one day at a time, one step at a time, trusting as you go. I can't wait for you to see what I have in store! Be expectant, for you have much to be excited about. Do not fear. The enemy will attempt to create confusion and doubt in you, but remember that he is a liar. Lean on my truth and worry about nothing. I have each and every detail under control. Exhale anxiety and inhale my peace. I'm calling you forward on this journey, my precious one. Hold my hand as I guide you with my counsel. Our adventure awaits. Are you ready?

Scripture

Jeremiah 29:11 "For I know the plans I have for you," declares the Lord, "plans to prosper you and not to harm you, plans to give you hope and a future."

Romans 8:28 And we know that in all things God works for the good of those who love him, who have been called according to his purpose.

Psalm 73:23-24 Yet I am always with you; you hold me by my right hand. You guide me with your counsel, and afterward you will take me into glory.

Psalm 37:23 (KJV) The steps of a good man are ordered by the Lord: and he delighteth in his way.

Isaiah 43:18-19 Forget the former things; do not dwell on the past. See, I am doing a new thing! Now it springs up; do you not perceive it? I am making a way in the wilderness and streams in the wasteland.

Psalm 138:8 (ESV) The Lord will fulfill his purpose for me; your steadfast love, O Lord, endures forever. Do not forsake the work of your hands.

I hear God whispering...

_____

_____

_____

_____

_____

_____

_____

_____

_____

_____

_____

_____

_____

_____

_____

_____

_____

DAY 2
JUST AS YOU ARE

I know you sometimes feel as though you must clean yourself up before drawing close to me, but please understand that's not the case. I am in the business of restoring and renewing hearts and minds. I want you to run to me exactly as you are. Let me meet you in your mess. Once you've asked me for forgiveness, I no longer remember the mistakes you've made, be it five years ago or five minutes ago. I love you with an everlasting love that cannot be altered. You must realize that my house isn't a country club for the elite, it's a hospital for the sick, and I'm your Great Physician. You can't clean yourself up alone. If you could, I wouldn't have had to send my son to die for you. Let my love transform you from the inside out like nothing else can. Come, just as you are. My arms are open wide.

Scripture

Romans 3:23-24 ...for all have sinned and fall short of the glory of God, and all are justified freely by his grace through the redemption that came by Christ Jesus.

Isaiah 64:6 (NLT) We are all infected and impure with sin. When we display our righteous deeds, they are nothing but filthy rags. Like autumn leaves, we wither and fall, and our sins sweep us away like the wind.

John 3:16-17 For God so loved the world that he gave his one and only Son, that whoever believes in him shall not perish but have eternal life. For God did not send his Son into the world to condemn the world, but to save the world through him.

John 15:3 (ESV) Already you are clean because of the word that I have spoken to you.

Romans 8:1-2 Therefore, there is now no condemnation for those who are in Christ Jesus, because through Christ Jesus the law of the Spirit who gives life has set you free from the law of sin and death.

I hear God whispering...

_____

_____

_____

_____

_____

_____

_____

_____

_____

_____

_____

_____

_____

_____

_____

_____

_____

_____

_____

DAY 3
LISTEN CLOSELY

Yes, dear one, you *can* hear my voice. I know you sometimes feel like others can hear me, but you aren't sure if you are able to. You wonder if the thoughts and ideas inside are coming from you or from me. I assure you, I'm speaking to you. I speak through my Holy Spirit and my Word. I whisper to you through sermons, songs, nature, and other people. Don't doubt your ability to hear me. Take time to listen. I love to hear your praises and thanksgiving as well as your requests, but allow me ample time to speak to you, too. It's a conversation in which both of us have dialogue. Like any relationship, it takes time and effort to get to know one another. Let's take turns speaking and listening. Make room and make time. Be confident in the fact that you can hear my voice. I'm speaking even now.

Scripture

John 10:27 (KJV) My sheep hear my voice, and I know them, and they follow me.

Jeremiah 33:3 Call to me and I will answer you and tell you great and unsearchable things you do not know.

John 14:26 (ESV) But the Helper, the Holy Spirit, whom the Father will send in my name, he will teach you all things and bring to your remembrance all that I have said to you.

Psalm 85:8 (ESV) Let me hear what God the Lord will speak, for he will speak peace to his people, to his saints; but let them not turn back to folly.

I hear God whispering...

_____

_____

_____

_____

_____

_____

_____

_____

_____

_____

_____

_____

_____

_____

_____

_____

_____

_____

DAY 4
STEADFAST LOVE

Do you know just how much I love you? I care about every single detail of your life. I know how many hairs are on your head and I've collected and numbered each tear you've ever cried. I sent my very son to earth as a sacrifice to ensure your freedom and your future. That's love! There's nothing you could ever do to lose it. My love is steadfast and overflowing at all times. I AM love. I fight for you and defend you in battles you're not even aware of. My protection wraps around you as a shield. I am yours and you are mine. May my whisper of, "I love you, Beloved" sweep away the worries of your day and remind you that the same God who hung the stars and tells the oceans where to stop, is desperately in love with you.

Scripture

Lamentation 3:22-23 (ESV) The steadfast love of the Lord never ceases; his mercies never come to an end; they are new every morning; great is your faithfulness.

Psalm 36:7 How priceless is your unfailing love, O God! People take refuge in the shadow of your wings.

Psalm 136:26 (NLT) Give thanks to the God of heaven. His faithful love endures forever.

Romans 5:8 (NLT) But God showed his great love for us by sending Christ to die for us while we were still sinners.

Luke 12:7 (ESV) Why, even the hairs of your head are all numbered. Fear not; you are of more value than many sparrows.

Psalm 56:8 (NLT) You keep track of all my sorrows. You have collected all my tears in your bottle. You have recorded each one in your book.

I hear God whispering...

DAY 5
BUT FIRST, PRAY

Prayer should always be your first response, not your last resort. It's easy to become overwhelmed by a circumstance and forget that I'm right here, waiting for you to come to me for help. You panic, you reach out to your family and friends, you try everything in your power to fix the problem and once you've exhausted all of your own ideas, you remember me. Come to me first, so I can guide and direct you in what to do. Pray to me and I'll give you peace and calm in the midst of confusion. I will make your paths straight and infuse you with clarity and discernment. Prayer is more powerful than you realize, precious one. This life isn't meant for you to figure out alone. I am with you always and I hear every word you pray. Bring your burdens to me first and feel my peace rush over you like a river. I'm just a breath away.

Scripture

Hebrews 4:16 (NLT) So let us come boldly to the throne of our gracious God. There we will receive his mercy, and we will find grace to help us when we need it most.

Psalm 145:18 (ISV) The Lord remains near to all who call out to him, to everyone who calls out to him sincerely.

---

1 Thessalonians 5:17 (NLT) Never stop praying.

Psalm 29:11 The Lord gives strength to his people; the Lord blesses his people with peace.

James 1:5 (NLT) If you need wisdom, ask our generous God, and he will give it to you. He will not rebuke you for asking.

Proverbs 3:6 (ISV) In all your ways acknowledge him, and he will make your paths straight.

I hear God whispering...

_____

_____

_____

_____

_____

_____

_____

_____

_____

_____

_____

_____

_____

_____

_____

_____

_____

_____

DAY 6
ON PURPOSE WITH PURPOSE

My beloved child, I took my careful time intricately knitting you together in your mother's womb. I chose the color of your eyes, your height, and every freckle, and I called you beautiful. You are perfect in my sight, for I do not make mistakes. You are precisely how I created you to be, full of passions and gifts, talents and desires, not one placed there by accident. You were made on purpose with purpose. Never forget that. Your calling is attached to who I made you to be. Look in the mirror and smile at my exquisite masterpiece. You are precious in my sight. Move forward in the bold confidence I freely give, and fulfill the destiny I handpicked especially for you. Do not be afraid, for I am with you wherever you go.

Scripture

Psalm 139:13-14 For you created my inmost being; you knit me together in my mother's womb. I praise you because I am fearfully and wonderfully made; your works are wonderful, I know that full well.

Jeremiah 1:5 Before I formed you in the womb I knew you, before you were born I set you apart; I appointed you as a prophet to the nations.

Ephesians 2:10 (NLT) For we are God's masterpiece. He has created us anew in Christ Jesus, so we can do the good things he planned for us long ago.

Song of Solomon 4:7 You are altogether beautiful, my darling; there is no flaw in you.

Genesis 1:27 (NLT) So God created human beings in his own image. In the image of God he created them; male and female he created them.

1 Peter 2:9 But you are a chosen people, a royal priesthood, a holy nation, God's special possession, that you may declare the praises of him who called you out of darkness into his wonderful light.

I hear God whispering...

_____

_____

_____

_____

_____

_____

_____

_____

_____

_____

_____

_____

_____

_____

_____

_____

_____

DAY 7
I AM

All that you will ever long for me to be, I Am. No matter your situation, my great name is available for you to call upon and ready to provide for your specific need. You have constant access. Do you require an Answer? I Am. A Provider? I Am. A Way-Maker? I Am. Do you need a Defender, a Faithful Friend, a Deliverer? Are you looking for a Healer, a Guide, a Protector, a Rest-Giver? Here I am. I shall be your Abba Father, your Burden-Bearer, Comforter, Vindicator, and Strong Tower. I'm your Song, your Strength, and your Prince of Peace. Call on me for your every need. I will be all you ask for and more. My name is matchless, above all other names. What do you need me to be for you today? Just ask. I Am that I Am.

Scripture

Exodus 3:12-14 (NLT) God answered, "I will be with you. And this is your sign that I am the one who has sent you: When you have brought the people out of Egypt, you will worship God at this very mountain." But Moses protested, "If I go to the people of Israel and tell them, 'The God of your ancestors has sent me to you,' they will ask me, 'What is his name?' Then what should I tell them?" God replied to Moses, "I Am who I Am. Say this to the people of Israel: I Am has sent me to you."

Jeremiah 8:18 You who are my Comforter in sorrow, my heart is faint within me.

Isaiah 9:6 For to us a child is born, to us a son is given, and the government will be on his shoulders. And he will be called Wonderful Counselor, Mighty God, Everlasting Father, Prince of Peace.

Psalm 48:14 For this God is our God for ever and ever; he will be our guide even to the end.

Isaiah 12:2 (NLT) See, God has come to save me. I will trust in him and not be afraid. The Lord God is my strength and my song; he has given me victory.

I hear God whispering...

_____
_____
_____
_____
_____
_____
_____
_____
_____
_____
_____
_____
_____
_____
_____
_____
_____
_____

DAY 8
SPEAK LIFE

Sons and daughters, the words you speak are extremely power-ful. They kill and they give life, they can build up and they can destroy. You have the freedom to choose how to use your words. My spoken words brought this very world into being. When I said, "Let there be...," there was. Whatever I say aloud becomes reality. Speak blessings, love, and encouragement. Declare the scriptures, my Word, with your mouth. You have the power to actually speak things into existence. Instead of saying, "I'll never be healed," use your voice to thank me in advance for your healing. Instead of using your words to tell others how people hurt you, use your words to pray for them instead. Employ wisdom when you choose what to say. Words coupled with faith can't be stopped!

Scripture

Proverbs 18:21 (ISV) The power of the tongue is life and death— those who love to talk will eat what it produces.

Genesis 1:3 (NLT) Then God said, "Let there be light," and there was light.

Mark 11:23 Truly I tell you, if anyone says to this mountain, 'Go, throw yourself into the sea,' and does not doubt in their heart but believes that what they say will happen, it will be done for them.

Colossians 4:6 (NLT) Let your conversation be gracious and attractive so that you will have the right response for everyone.

Ephesians 4:29 Do not let any unwholesome talk come out of your mouths, but only what is helpful for building others up according to their needs, that it may benefit those who listen.

Psalm 141:3 (NLT) Take control of what I say, O Lord, and guard my lips.

I hear God whispering...

_____

_____

_____

_____

_____

_____

_____

_____

_____

_____

_____

_____

_____

_____

_____

_____

_____

DAY 9
ON SCHEDULE

My timing is perfect. It always has been and it always will be. As the creator and holder of time, I make all things beautiful at precisely the right moment. My timing in your life is absolutely imperative. I orchestrate divinely scheduled appointments, helping you arrive to a particular destination "for such a time as this." If I tell you to go, move quickly! I have eyes to see what you can't. You mustn't hesitate when I give you an instruction. My protection, my provision, and my favor are all connected to the timing of your obedience. Are you still waiting on a prayer to be answered? Trust me and my perfect timing. Don't let time cause you to doubt what I've told you would happen. I'm never early; I'm never late. My answers are always on schedule. Be still and know that I will forever be right on time from now until eternity. I hold every piece of your world in my hands.

Scripture

Ecclesiastes 3:11 (NLT) Yet God has made everything beautiful for its own time. He has planted eternity in the human heart, but even so, people cannot see the whole scope of God's work from beginning to end.

Acts 1:7 He said to them: "It is not for you to know the times or dates the Father has set by his own authority."

Psalm 90:4 (NLT) For you, a thousand years are as a passing day, as brief as a few night hours.

---

2 Peter 3:8 But do not forget this one thing, dear friends: With the Lord a day is like a thousand years, and a thousand years are like a day.

I hear God whispering...

_____

_____

_____

_____

_____

_____

_____

_____

_____

_____

_____

_____

_____

_____

_____

_____

_____

DAY 10
YOUR GOOD FATHER

My child, believe me when I tell you that worrying is "for the birds" and my Word says that they don't even worry because I look after and provide for them. How much more do I care about you? You're worth far more to me than the birds of the air. I created you in my image. I am Jehovah-Jireh, your provider. I will supply every need you have, for it's in my very nature to be faithful to you. When a child asks her father for food, does he give her a rock? No! If a sinful parent can give a child good gifts, think how much more I, your heavenly Father, can give the most wonderfully good gifts to my children. Rely on me for all you need and watch as I supply that and abundantly more. I'm your good Father and I will never disappoint you.

Scripture

Matthew 6:26 (NLT) Look at the birds. They don't plant or harvest or store food in barns, for your heavenly Father feeds them. And aren't you far more valuable to him than they are?

Philippians 4:19 And my God will meet all your needs according to the riches of His glory in Christ Jesus.

Matthew 6:31-33 (NLT) So don't worry about these things, saying, "What will we eat? What will we drink? What will we wear?" These things dominate the thoughts of unbelievers, but your heavenly Father already knows all your needs. Seek the Kingdom of God above all else, and live righteously, and he will give you everything you need.

Matthew 7:11 If you, then, though you are evil, know how to give good gifts to your children, how much more will your Father in heaven give good gifts to those who ask him!

I hear God whispering...

_____

_____

_____

_____

_____

_____

_____

_____

_____

_____

_____

_____

_____

_____

_____

_____

_____

_____

DAY 11
MY POWER IS YOURS

Sons and daughters, trust and believe that I have all power in my hands. I shaped the mountains and parted the seas. I healed the sick and calmed the storms. Have you ever stopped for a moment to think about just how powerful I am? And what's more, the same power that raised my son from the grave lives inside of YOU. Because I live in you, there is no limit to what you can do! I tell you the truth, if you believe, you will do the same works Christ has done and even greater things. Call forth miracles, signs, and wonders in the name of Jesus and be amazed. All will stare wide-eyed in disbelief because of your limitless faith and my limitless power. Claim it and change the world!

Scripture

Romans 8:11 (NLT) The Spirit of God, who raised Jesus from the dead, lives in you. And just as God raised Christ Jesus from the dead, he will give life to your mortal bodies by this same Spirit living within you.

John 14:12 Very truly I tell you, whoever believes in me will do the works I have been doing, and they will do even greater things than these, because I am going to the Father.

Psalm 107:29 He stilled the storm to a whisper; the waves of the sea were hushed.

Amos 4:13 He who forms the mountains, who creates the wind, and who reveals his thoughts to mankind, who turns dawn to darkness, and treads on the heights of the earth- the Lord God Almighty is his name.

Psalm 95:4 (NLT) He holds in his hands the depths of the earth and the mightiest mountains.

I hear God whispering...

_____

_____

_____

_____

_____

_____

_____

_____

_____

_____

_____

_____

_____

_____

_____

_____

DAY 12
PRESS ON

Keep moving forward, one step at a time. No matter what you see with your natural eyes, press on. Faith, not sight, my precious one. I'm with you, holding your hand as we run together atop mountains and through valleys. I never promised a life free from difficult days, but I did promise to walk with you through them. I supply all you need, every moment of every day. Are you weak? Your weakness is made perfect in my strength. Are you tired? I will refresh the weary and satisfy the faint. Are you worried? Pray and receive my peace, which passes understanding. I know it gets tough, but do not grow weary in well doing, for at just the right time, you'll see your harvest. Hold fast and stay the course, my hand in yours. Onward we march.

Scripture

2 Corinthians 12:9 (NLT) Each time he said, "My grace is all you need. My power works best in weakness." So now I am glad to boast about my weaknesses, so that the power of Christ can work through me.

Galatians 6:9 Let us not become weary in doing good, for at the proper time we will reap a harvest if we do not give up.

Jeremiah 31:25 I will refresh the weary and satisfy the faint.

Hebrews 10:36 You need to persevere so that when you have done the will of God, you will receive what he has promised.

I hear God whispering...

_____

_____

_____

_____

_____

_____

_____

_____

_____

_____

_____

_____

_____

_____

_____

_____

_____

_____

DAY 13
FREEDOM IN FORGIVENESS

Today I ask you to search yourself for any lingering bitterness, hurt, or unforgiveness. Are there remnants of an offense still latched onto your heart? I know it hurt and trust me when I tell you I know how it feels. I came to earth in the person of my son and experienced injustice, torture, ridicule, and abuse. As impossible as it may seem, I ask you to forgive those who have wronged you. Let them off of your hook, knowing that I am just and I am El Roi, the God who sees. Forgiveness is not for the offender's sake, it's for yours. When you forgive, you experience total freedom, as bitterness melts away and a dark heaviness is lifted from you, creating the bliss of total inner peace. I forgive you endlessly. Jesus died so that you could be forgiven. You must forgive also. Leave your past and your hurts in my hands today and live in carefree freedom.

Scripture

Colossians 3:13 Bear with each other and forgive one another if any of you has a grievance against someone. Forgive as the Lord forgave you.

Ephesians 4:31-32 (NLT) Get rid of all bitterness, rage, anger, harsh words, and slander, as well as all types of evil behavior. Instead, be kind to each other, tenderhearted, forgiving one another, just as God through Christ has forgiven you.

Hebrews 10:30 For we know him who said, "It is mine to avenge; I will repay," and again, "The Lord will judge his people."

Genesis 16:13 (ESV) So she called the name of the Lord who spoke to her, "You are a God of seeing," for she said, "Truly here I have seen him who looks after me."

I hear God whispering...

DAY 14
PROMISE KEEPER

I am a promise maker and a promise keeper and I promise you my Word will never return void. I cannot lie, so all that I've said about you and all that I've said to you will most assuredly come to pass. I will keep my Word and see it through. I have every resource available at my fingertips. I can move mountains and I can change hearts. With a snap of my fingers or a whisper from my lips, anything can happen, for nothing is impossible for me. Cling to my promises and whatever you do, never stop believing. I can do all things but fail you. Stand on my unchanging Word as you watch my promises appear before your very eyes. You can count on the fact that I will always come through.

Scripture

Psalm 145:13 Your kingdom is an everlasting kingdom, and your dominion endures through all generations. The Lord is trustworthy in all he promises and faithful in all he does.

Deuteronomy 7:9 Know therefore that the Lord your God is God; he is the faithful God, keeping his covenant of love to a thousand generations of those who love him and keep his commandments.

2 Timothy 2:13 (ISV) Our faith may fail, his never wanes- That's who he is, he cannot change!

2 Corinthians 1:20 (ISV) For all God's promises are "Yes" in him. And so through him we can say "Amen," to the glory of God.

Isaiah 55:11 (KJV) So shall my word be that goeth forth out of my mouth: it shall not return unto me void, but it shall accomplish that which I please, and it shall prosper in the thing whereto I sent it.

I hear God whispering...

DAY 15
DON'T FORCE IT

Sweet child, you never have to frantically force anything to happen. Be obedient in what I tell you to do, but let me do the heavy lifting. My yoke is easy and my burden is light. I'm the expert. As the architect, I've created the blueprint, so leave it to me. Keep working with excellence on what I've currently set before you to do, and know that I've given you the confidence, peace, confirmations, and joy regarding what I have in store. In due time and in my perfect way, I will make it happen. *I* will take care of the "how." Do you trust me to open the right doors and align you with the right people and opportunities? Do you trust me to be in all of the details? Don't try to manipulate situations to force your prayers to be answered. Please don't do it on your own. It's my job and my pleasure. I know when and how is best. Trust your loving Father.

Scripture

Matthew 11:30 For my yoke is easy and my burden is light.

Ephesians 3:16 I pray that out of his glorious riches he may strengthen you with power through his Spirit in your inner being.

Psalm 77:14 (MSG) You're the God who makes things happen; you showed everyone what you can do-

Philippians 1:6 being confident of this, that he who began a good work in you will carry it on to completion until the day of Christ Jesus.

Exodus 14:14 The Lord will fight for you; you need only to be still.

Psalm 37:5 (ESV) Commit your way to the Lord; trust in him, and he will act.

I hear God whispering...

DAY 16
A GRATEFUL HEART

Oh, how I love to hear you give thanks. I beam over your "thank-you" as I answer big prayers and move mountains in your life, but truly I tell you, there is nothing too small for thanksgiving. Thank me throughout your day, every day. Give me thanks for a prime parking place, for a green light when you're running late, and for your favorite song coming on the radio. When you thank me for the things you see as small or insignificant in addition to your "big" answered prayers, you'll soon realize just how blessed you are. Thanksgiving won't ever leave your lips! When you're tempted to complain, begin to thank me for my many blessings instead. Sit down and compose a list and watch it grow! Your perspective will soon change and my goodness will wash over you, filling your heart with overwhelming gratitude.

Scripture

Jeremiah 30:19 (ISV) Thanksgiving and the sounds of laughter will come out of them. I'll cause them to increase in numbers and not decrease. I'll honor them and not make them insignificant.

---

2 Chronicles 5:13 (NLT) The trumpeters and singers performed together in unison to praise and give thanks to the Lord. Accompanied by trumpets, cymbals, and other instruments, they raised their voices and praised the Lord with these words: "He is good! His faithful love endures forever!" At that moment a thick cloud filled the Temple of the Lord.

Psalm 107:8-9 (NLT) Let them praise the Lord for his great love and for the wonderful things he has done for them. For he satisfies the thirsty and fills the hungry with good things.

Psalm 95:2 (ISV) Let us come into his presence with thanksgiving; let us shout with songs of praise to him.

---

1 Chronicles 16:34 Give thanks to the Lord, for he is good; his love endures forever.

I hear God whispering...

_____

_____

_____

_____

_____

_____

_____

_____

_____

_____

_____

_____

_____

_____

_____

_____

DAY 17
SOW MY SEEDS

I am strategic in who I place on your path. No one is ever there by chance. You either learn from, or influence each person I put in your life. Show my unconditional love and be a beacon of my light to all those around you. See others how I see them, through my eyes. Sow seeds of faith, joy, time, prayer, and financial blessings into everyone I've introduced to you. Not one thing that you do for others or for me is ever in vain. I waste nothing! Sometimes I'll allow you to see what your planted seeds have brought forth and other times you'll never know, but be confident that you are a vital part of many faith stories. You're in charge of sowing, but I'm in charge of the results of the harvest. When you join me in heaven, you'll get to see just how many lives I allowed you to touch whether you realized it or not. Go now and be my hands and feet to those around you. You are blessed to be a blessing.

Scripture

1 John 4:11 (NLT) Dear friends, since God loved us that much, we surely ought to love each other.

Romans 12:10 Be devoted to one another in love. Honor one another above yourselves.

---

1 John 4:7-8 (ESV) Beloved, let us love one another, for love is from God, and whoever loves has been born of God and knows God. Anyone who does not love does not know God, because God is love.

Luke 6:31 Do to others as you would have them do to you.

John 15:12 (ESV) This is my commandment, that you love one another as I have loved you.

Ephesians 4:32 (ESV) Be kind to one another, tenderhearted, forgiving one another, as God in Christ forgave you.

I hear God whispering...

_____

_____

_____

_____

_____

_____

_____

_____

_____

_____

_____

_____

_____

_____

_____

_____

_____

DAY 18
JOY DESPITE CIRCUMSTANCES

My dearest, I understand how easy it is to look at your circumstances and get overwhelmed by how you feel. Be reminded today, however, that feelings can lie and are fleeting like the wind. Stand on the One who is your steadfast Rock. I am unchanging, sturdy, and safe at all times. You may feel discouraged and frustrated. Things may look bleak with your natural eyes, but what you see happening should not determine your joy. Disappointment may bring tears, but worship me nevertheless! Praise me no matter how you feel. The enemy comes to steal, kill, and destroy, and he loves to take your joy. Hold it close! Press into me, moving your feelings aside to see that I am your steadfast God who supplies *lasting* joy despite your circumstances. My joy is your strength.

Scripture

Jeremiah 17:9 (ISV) The heart is more deceitful than anything. It is incurable- who can know it?

Psalm 46:1 God is our refuge and strength, an ever-present help in trouble.

Psalm 34:1-3 (TLB) I will praise the Lord no matter what happens. I will constantly speak of his glories and grace. I will boast of all his kindness to me. Let all who are discouraged take heart. Let us praise the Lord together and exalt his name.

John 10:10 The thief comes only to steal and kill and destroy; I have come that they may have life, and have it to the full.

Nehemiah 8:10 (ISV) He also told them, "Go eat the best food, drink the best wine, and give something to those who have nothing, since this day is holy to our Lord. Don't be sorrowful, because the joy of the Lord is your strength."

I hear God whispering...

_____

_____

_____

_____

_____

_____

_____

_____

_____

_____

_____

_____

_____

_____

_____

_____

DAY 19
YOUR UNCHANGING ROCK

You live in a world that is constantly changing. Trends come and go and people walk in and out of your life. Minds change as often as the weather changes. Sometimes you feel as if you're walking on shifting sand, wondering where to plant your foot for its next sturdy step. Remember, I am your constant, solid rock. I am unchanging- the same yesterday, today, and forever. What I have spoken will be fulfilled, for I cannot lie. I am your foundation that cannot be shaken and I will never leave you nor forsake you. Though the waves crash and the winds blow, you will not be moved. I hold your beginning and your end for I am the Alpha and the Omega. Despite the changes all around you, place your hope and trust in the One who cannot change.

Scripture

Numbers 23:19 God is not human, that he should lie, not a human being, that he should change his mind. Does he speak and then not act? Does he promise and not fulfill?

Hebrews 13:8 Jesus Christ is the same yesterday and today and forever.

Malachi 3:6 (NLT) I am the Lord, and I do not change. That is why you descendants of Jacob are not already destroyed.

Revelation 22:13 I am the Alpha and the Omega, the First and the Last, the Beginning and the End.

Deuteronomy 31:6 Be strong and courageous. Do not be afraid or terrified because of them, for the Lord your God goes with you; he will never leave you nor forsake you."

Isaiah 26:4 (ESV) Trust in the Lord forever, for the Lord God is an everlasting rock.

I hear God whispering...

_____
_____
_____
_____
_____
_____
_____
_____
_____
_____
_____
_____
_____
_____
_____
_____
_____
_____
_____

DAY 20
WELL DONE

Yes child, I see all and know all. I'm omniscient and omnipresent so I never miss a thing. I see your integrity when no one else is looking. Even the smallest gestures make me smile. I watch with delight as you consistently keep your word and show up on time, return someone else's shopping cart left in the parking lot, give back the money you see fall out of a pocket, and offer your time and resources to others expecting nothing in return. In a world where this is not the norm, I am so proud of how you live. When you don't hear the 'thank-you,' and you know no one is watching, realize that I see and I'm pleased. When you feel frustrated, longing for someone to be grateful for your efforts, listen as I whisper in your ear, "Well done my good and faithful servant." Continue going above and beyond, living your life with integrity, knowing that my approval is all that you need.

Scripture

Proverbs 21:3 (NLT) The Lord is more pleased when we do what is right and just than when we offer him sacrifices.

Luke 6:31 Do to others as you would have them do to you.

Psalm 41:12 Because of my integrity you uphold me and set me in your presence forever.

Matthew 25:21 His master replied, 'Well done, good and faithful servant! You have been faithful with a few things; I will put you in charge of many things. Come and share your master's happiness!'

Proverbs 15:3 (NLT) The Lord is watching everywhere, keeping his eye on both the evil and the good.

I hear God whispering...

_____

_____

_____

_____

_____

_____

_____

_____

_____

_____

_____

_____

_____

_____

_____

_____

_____

DAY 21
EMBRACE MY PROCESS

Dear one, I realize that it's human nature that makes you long to skip over the waiting period and get right to the blessing, the breakthrough, and the answered prayer, but there is much to be gained in the wait. You must learn to embrace my process. I am working more than you can imagine during this necessary time, not only preparing the circumstances around you, but also maturing, pruning, and preparing you for the very thing you've been praying for. If I gave you what you asked for immediately, how would your faith ever grow? Would you even be ready to handle it? You must be placed in seasons of waiting as you learn to fully lean on and trust in me. Be content in the process, knowing that I'm working in and through you, readying you for the wonderfully incredible plans I have for your future.

Scripture

Psalm 27:14 (NLT) Wait patiently for the Lord. Be brave and courageous. Yes, wait patiently for the Lord.

Psalm 33:20 We wait in hope for the Lord; he is our help and our shield.

Micah 7:7 (ESV) But as for me, I will look to the Lord; I will wait for the God of my salvation; my God will hear me.

Romans 4:18-21 Against all hope, Abraham in hope believed and so became the father of many nations, just as it had been said to him, "So shall your offspring be." Without weakening in his faith, he faced the fact that his body was as good as dead- since he was about a hundred years old- and that Sarah's womb was also dead. Yet he did not waver through unbelief regarding the promise of God, but was strengthened in his faith and gave glory to God, being fully persuaded that God had power to do what he had promised.

I hear God whispering...

DAY 22
DRAW NEAR

I long for your undivided attention, my love. You are constantly bombarded by distractions competing for your time, but what will you choose to run after? I, your heavenly Father, the King of the Universe, pursue you moment by moment and desire your reciprocated pursuit of me. I love to be sought after by my children. I never play games of hide-and-seek, rather I delight in drawing near to you as you draw near to me. Seek me through prayer, worship, serving, giving, time, and talents- not just on Sundays, but every day. Let pursuing your Father become a life-style. You can always seek me for what you need, but seek me first because my presence is enough and I'm worth it. Make room for me, the One who promises to never stop running after you. I love you so much. Draw near.

Scripture

Deuteronomy 4:29 (ISV) If from there you will seek the Lord your God, then you will find him if you seek him with all your heart and soul.

Proverbs 8:17 I love those who love me, and those who seek me find me.

1 Chronicles 16:11 (ESV) Seek the Lord and his strength; seek his presence continually!

Matthew 6:33 (NLT) Seek the Kingdom of God above all else, and live righteously, and he will give you everything you need.

I hear God whispering...

_____

_____

_____

_____

_____

_____

_____

_____

_____

_____

_____

_____

_____

_____

_____

_____

DAY 23
LET GO AND KNOW

Dear one, if I take something from you, know that I can only replace it with better. I give and take away, but continue to bless my name, believing that I'm your perfect Father who knows what's best for you. Come to me with your questions, disappointments, and confusion. I can handle it. I will love you through it. Open your spiritual eyes and remember that my ways and thoughts are higher than yours. I can see what you can't. I will restore to you the years that the locusts stole. Better is coming, in fact, better is here. Let go freely of what I'm asking for with an understanding that the best is yet to come. Watch for the beautiful gifts I have in store for you. Taste and see that I am good all the time.

Scripture

Job 1:21 (GNT) He said, "I was born with nothing, and I will die with nothing. The Lord gave, and now he has taken away. May his name be praised!"

Isaiah 55:8-9 (NLT) "My thoughts are nothing like your thoughts," says the Lord. "And my ways are far beyond anything you could imagine. For just as the heavens are higher than the earth, so my ways are higher than your ways and my thoughts higher than your thoughts.

Joel 2:25 (ESV) I will restore to you the years that the swarming locust has eaten, the hopper, the destroyer, and the cutter, my great army, which I sent among you.

1 Corinthians 2:9 (ISV) But as it is written, "No eye has seen, no ear has heard, and no mind has imagined the things that God has prepared for those who love him."

Psalm 34:8 (ISV) Taste and see that the LORD is good! How blessed is the person who trusts in him!

I hear God whispering...

_____
_____
_____
_____
_____
_____
_____
_____
_____
_____
_____
_____
_____
_____
_____
_____
_____
_____

DAY 24
SMALL VICTORIES

I know the dreams in your heart, for they were placed there by me. It's so easy to disregard what you see as "small" milestones along your journey because you're so focused on attaining the end result. Today, I want you to praise me for each and every part of your adventure with me. When you appreciate the small things, it makes me want to give you abundantly more. Celebrate no matter how seemingly insignificant they appear to you. I will use them all as preparation to set up the scene for the grand finale. Enjoy the season I have you in, as well. Don't wish it away. You may never see another one like it. If it's a season of rest, rest. If it's a season of growth, grow. Each one is so significant and necessary for your next assignment. It's fun to look forward to what I have promised you, but enjoy each stop along the way. Be thankful and know that I'll get you there right on time. You have my word.

Scripture

Psalm 9:1 (ESV) I will give thanks to the Lord with my whole heart; I will recount all of your wonderful deeds.

Luke 16:10 (NLT) If you are faithful in little things, you will be faithful in large ones. But if you are dishonest in little things, you won't be honest with greater responsibilities.

Zechariah 4:10 (NLT) Do not despise these small beginnings, for the Lord rejoices to see the work begin, to see the plumb line in Zerubbabel's hand..."

Isaiah 60:22 (ISV) The least of them will become a thousand, and the smallest one a mighty nation. "I am the Lord; When the time is right, I will do this swiftly."

I hear God whispering...

_____
_____
_____
_____
_____
_____
_____
_____
_____
_____
_____
_____
_____
_____
_____
_____
_____

DAY 25
HELP ME OVERCOME
MY UNBELIEF

Beloved, know that I understand the limitations of your humanity.
Your mind can only comprehend so much, but I ask you to believe me
with every fiber of your being. The father of the tormented son in the gos-
pel of Mark said the famous words, "I do believe, help me overcome my
unbelief." This profound request resonates inside of you. Deep down, you
believe and know that I have the power and ability to do anything, but you
wonder if I actually will. Don't beat yourself up for questioning me or for
feeling disappointment and frustration when doubt creeps in. You are but
human. Quickly confess and repent to me, asking for my help to refocus
your heart and recalibrate your thoughts to sync up with mine. When you
can't see and you feel overwhelmed and discouraged, claim your belief
and ask for my help to banish any residue of doubt. Weeping may last for a
night, but joy comes in the morning. I will always help you overcome your
unbelief. You need only ask.

Scripture

Mark 9:21-24 Jesus asked the boy's father, "How long has he been like this?" "From childhood," he answered. "It has often thrown him into fire or water to kill him. But if you can do anything, take pity on us and help us." "'If you can'?" said Jesus. "Everything is possible for one who believes." Immediately the boy's father exclaimed, "I do believe; help me overcome my unbelief!"

Psalm 30:5 (NLT) For his anger lasts only a moment, but his favor lasts a lifetime! Weeping may last through the night, but joy comes with the morning.

Acts 3:19 Repent, then, and turn to God, so that your sins may be wiped out, that times of refreshing may come from the Lord.

Hebrews 11:1 (NLT) Faith is the confidence that what we hope for will actually happen; it gives us assurance about things we cannot see.

Mark 11:24 Therefore I tell you, whatever you ask for in prayer, believe that you have received it, and it will be yours.

I hear God whispering...

DAY 26
CHANGING SEASONS

As you've come to realize over time, I operate in seasons. In your life, you will have friendships, jobs, churches, and dating relationships, to name a few, that are only meant for a particular amount of time. I understand that change can be difficult for you, but be assured that I know what you need in every stage of your life. There will be times when I ask you to make a change, when I ask for your yes of obedience and you can't comprehend why. It's okay! Trust me. I never said radical faith would always make sense. Maybe a season comes to an end because you have learned what was necessary or maybe because I'm protecting you from what you can't see. Maybe your season is concluding because I have a new assignment for you with abundantly more waiting right around the corner. No matter the purpose, cherish all of your seasons, but learn to trust me when they change. Believe with your whole heart that I have your best interest in mind every moment of your life.

Scripture

Psalm 139:16 (NLT) You saw me before I was born. Every day of my life was recorded in your book. Every moment was laid out before a single day had passed.

Psalm 104:19 He made the moon to mark the seasons, and the sun knows when to go down.

Proverbs 3:5-6 (ESV) Trust in the Lord with all your heart, and do not lean on your own understanding. In all your ways acknowledge him, and he will make straight your paths.

Ecclesiastes 3:1 (NLT) For everything there is a season, a time for every activity under heaven.

I hear God whispering...

_____

_____

_____

_____

_____

_____

_____

_____

_____

_____

_____

_____

_____

_____

_____

_____

_____

DAY 27
VICTORY IS OURS

I declare that no weapon formed against you will prosper. I am canceling the assignment of the enemy on your life at this very moment. Push forward unafraid, bold warrior. Speak my truth aloud at all times. My Word is your sword, your offensive weapon. Use it without hesitation. Keep it written on your heart and ready on your tongue. Remember my power resides in you. Just the whisper of my son's name on your lips makes demons flee and darkness tremble. Jesus. Say it aloud, "Jesus." You can always claim the victory because I've already won the war. You have the advantage of knowing the end of the story before it even happens, and let me remind you, it's a good one. Victory is forever ours!

Scripture

James 4:7 Submit yourselves, then, to God. Resist the devil, and he will flee from you.

1 Peter 5:8-9 (NLT) Stay alert! Watch out for your great enemy, the devil. He prowls around like a roaring lion, looking for someone to devour. Stand firm against him, and be strong in your faith. Remember that your family of believers all over the world is going through the same kind of suffering you are.

Isaiah 54:17 (NLT) But in that coming day no weapon turned against you will succeed. You will silence every voice raised up to accuse you. These benefits are enjoyed by the servants of the Lord; their vindication will come from me. I, the Lord, have spoken!

Ephesians 6:17 (NLT) Put on salvation as your helmet, and take the sword of the Spirit, which is the word of God.

Romans 8:37 (NLT) No, despite all these things, overwhelming victory is ours through Christ, who loved us.

Luke 10:17 (ESV) The seventy-two returned with joy, saying, "Lord, even the demons are subject to us in your name!"

I hear God whispering...

DAY 28
SALT AND LIGHT

I have handpicked you to live differently. You are called to be light in the darkness and salt to season this earth. Stand out and let your life make everyone around you want what you have: Me. Do not blend into this world, but shine so brightly that people see my smile in your smile and experience my love through your love. You must not mourn the fact that you don't fit in, but rejoice instead, because I have set you apart. This earth is not your home, child. Dare to be different. But take heed: I do not wish for you to shun, look down upon, and turn your back on this world, for how will they be shown my goodness? Love others unconditionally as you share my truth. Hate evil and cling to what is good. Go and make disciples. Burn with the fire of my Holy Spirit and stand out for my name's sake.

Scripture

Romans 12:2 (NLT) Don't copy the behavior and customs of this world, but let God transform you into a new person by changing the way you think. Then you will learn to know God's will for you, which is good and pleasing and perfect.

Matthew 5:13-16 (NLT) You are the salt of the earth. But what good is salt if it has lost its flavor? Can you make it salty again? It will be thrown out and trampled underfoot as worthless. You are the light of the world- like a city on a hilltop that cannot be hidden. No one lights a lamp and then puts it under a basket. Instead, a lamp is placed on a stand, where it gives light to everyone in the house. In the same way, let your good deeds shine out for all to see, so that everyone will praise your heavenly Father.

Hebrews 13:14 (NLT) For this world is not our permanent home; we are looking forward to a home yet to come.

1 John 2:17 (NLT) And this world is fading away, along with everything that people crave. But anyone who does what pleases God will live forever.

John 17:16 (ISV) They don't belong to the world, just as I don't belong to the world.

Romans 12:9 Love must be sincere. Hate what is evil; cling to what is good.

I hear God whispering...

DAY 29
PARADISE AWAITS

It won't be long until you are skipping on the streets of gold, worshipping alongside legions of angels, and feasting with me in paradise. I'm putting the final touches on a mansion with your name on it. Heaven is beyond your comprehension now, but it is as real as the ground you stand on. No eye has seen and no ear has heard what I'm preparing for you. The wolf and the lamb will feed together. The lame will leap and the blind will see. There will be no more death, tears, or pain. All things will be made new. It's too wonderful for you to imagine, even in your wildest dreams. Live in excited, expectant anticipation of my coming. Press on and remember that you're a vapor, here for the blink of an eye in the light of eternity. Make it count, for paradise awaits.

Scripture

1 Corinthians 2:9 (ISV) But as it is written, "No eye has seen, no ear has heard, and no mind has imagined the things that God has prepared for those who love him."

Isaiah 35: 5-6 (NLT) And when he comes, he will open the eyes of the blind and unplug the ears of the deaf. The lame will leap like a deer, and those who cannot speak will sing for joy! Springs will gush forth in the wilderness, and streams will water the wasteland.

Revelation 21:3-4 (NLT) I heard a loud shout from the throne, saying, "Look, God's home is now among his people! He will live with them, and they will be his people. God himself will be with them. He will wipe every tear from their eyes, and there will be no more death or sorrow or crying or pain. All these things are gone forever."

John 14:2-3 (NLT) There is more than enough room in my Father's home. If this were not so, would I have told you that I am going to prepare a place for you? When everything is ready, I will come and get you, so that you will always be with me where I am.

James 4:14 (ISV) You do not know what tomorrow will bring. What is your life? You are a mist that appears for a little while and then vanishes.

I hear God whispering...

_____

_____

_____

_____

_____

_____

_____

_____

_____

_____

_____

_____

_____

_____

_____

_____

DAY 30
CONTINUE MY PURSUIT

I'm so proud of you, my child. Thank you for carving room for me each day and for committing to meditate on my scripture and listen for my voice. I will forever be the King of your heart and I will continue to speak to you as you take time to be still and listen. Continue pursuing me and writing down what I whisper in your ear. Talk to me about anything and everything on your mind and then allow me the time to sing over you with my love, instruct you with my truth, and inspire you with my faithfulness. I will give you divine moments to bless and encourage others with the words I've spoken to you, as well. You are so special to me and the thought of you fills me with indescribable joy. I'm with you always and I eagerly await the day we will be face to face in paradise forever. Until then…

Scripture

Psalm 119:103 How sweet are your words to my taste, sweeter than honey to my mouth!

Romans 10:17 (ESV) So faith comes from hearing, and hearing through the word of Christ.

Jeremiah 33:3 Call to me and I will answer you and tell you great and unsearchable things you do not know.

John 10:27 (ESV) My sheep hear my voice, and I know them, and they follow me.

Psalm 34:10 The lions may grow weak and hungry, but those who seek the Lord lack no good thing.

Jeremiah 29:13 You will seek me and find me when you seek me with all your heart.

I hear God whispering...

_____

_____

_____

_____

_____

_____

_____

_____

_____

_____

_____

_____

_____

_____

_____

_____

_____

_____

PRAYER

If you've never officially given your heart to Jesus and you're ready to make the best decision of your life, pray this prayer:

Lord Jesus, I believe you died on the cross for me and I can never thank you enough. Forgive me for my sins and remember them no more. I ask you to come into my life today. I receive you as my Lord and Savior and ask that you help me live with joy for you the rest of my life. Thank you for who you are, for what you've done, and for what you're doing now and forever. Today I am made new. Amen.

Mark this date on your calendar! Please let me know about your exciting decision. I want to celebrate with you!

Email: hello@mellieboozer.com

ACKNOWLEDGEMENTS

My very first acknowledgement of gratitude has to go to my Heavenly Father. Thank you, God, for being big enough to scatter the stars in the sky, yet small enough to whisper in my ear. Thank you for sending my Savior, Jesus, and my Guide, the Holy Spirit, and for helping me achieve a dream I didn't even know I had. This book is for you. All glory and honor and praise are yours forever.

Mom and Dad, thank you for being living, breathing examples of unconditional love and extraordinary generosity. Huge thanks for constantly believing in me and raising me in the faith. I am forever grateful.

Tori, you are the best sister on earth! I thank you so much for speaking truth to me always and inspiring me daily. I truly appreciate you helping me so much throughout this process and for being my very first editor, too.

To my grandmothers, Mimi (Nell) and Goggy (Millie), and to my Great-Aunt Glenda, I definitely have to acknowledge you three for being the most amazing role models throughout my life. Thank you to all of my incredible family for your unending support and love.

To my cousin, Jessica, and to Pastor Jackie, I'm so thankful that you challenged me, unbeknownst to each other, to take time and write down what God was whispering to me. This book is the result of your obedience to speak what He told you to.

Esther, I offer my heartfelt thanks for believing in what God wants to do with this book. Your selflessness, prayers, investment, and love have been beyond appreciated and I am truly thankful.

Bridgette, thank you for your constant encouragement and consistent prayers. You are an inspiration and a Godsend in my life.

Ashley, I can't thank you enough for pouring into me and allowing me to be a part of the Hidden Truth Jewelry ministry. You are an answer to prayer, dear friend.

Kristie and Jordan, I am forever blessed to call you my ride-or-die BFFs and I thank you for your support, help, and love during this process and always. Cue me putting on my bird necklace.

Carol, I absolutely have to thank you for sitting beside me in the acting workshop and unknowingly being part of God's awesome plan of weaving lives together for reasons we couldn't even dream of. Thank you for allowing me to use your gorgeous painting for my cover.

Katie, thanks so much for professionally photographing the cover painting, for dancing with me at all times, and for being just as passionate about "the journey" as I am.

Jerry, thank you for your phenomenal job helping me figure out what I wanted my cover to look like. I'm so proud of what we created. The patience and time you gave me will never be forgotten. In addition, Shane, thank you for being editor extraordinaire!

Alex, thanks so much for shooting my Kickstarter video, for giving me super helpful advice, and for being an unbelievably talented and precious friend.

Jamesha, thank you for being just perfect in my Kickstarter video. I'm sincerely grateful for all of the times you've spoken life and truth into me and reminded me of God's promises.

To my pastors, Travis and Jackie Greene, thank you beyond words for planting Forward City Church and for pushing me out of my comfort zone and into a deeper relationship with Christ. Thanks for loving and encouraging me and for being such wonderful leaders and friends. Big thanks to my FCC family, as well, for inspiring me constantly. Of course I can't forget to thank the Chili Peppers. You already know!

Leighton, thank you for your faithful prayers and loving, powerful words. You're amazing. Thanks also to the Post College Spiritual Sistas for being my wonderfully encouraging first readers.

Crystal and Shomoneik, I thank you for your special friendship, for your steadfast encouragement, and for your love.

Kadie, thank you for being the first person years ago to tell me that I should write a devotional book. Thank you for creating my author website, too! You're an incredible friend and a forever sister.

To Liz, Vanessa, Falon, Janaé, Katherine, & Jaméz, I thank you all for speaking life into me and for your faithful prayers.

Jennifer, thank you for sitting down with me patiently in the very beginning when God had given me this idea. The way you explained the self-publishing process was so helpful and your advice was invaluable. May you continue to succeed and help others to do the same.

To my Kickstarter backers, my heartfelt gratitude goes out to each and every one of you who helped bring this book to life! Special thanks to the following: Dawn Darby, Terry Reid, Tony & Sally Brown, Jennifer Stewart, Christina Coleman, Elizabeth Krawczyk, Jaméz Fletcher, LuAnn Washington, LGM Moore, Cindy Zwolensky, Ashley Weston, Vanessa Harper, Latan Cox, Jim and Lynda Keisler, Nan Coghill, Amy Hebert, Rick and Sandy Hurst, Allison Tocci, Linda Amick, and Ben and Kristie Angstadt. I am forever grateful!

Finally, I thank YOU for giving this little book a chance. I pray you were blessed through this journey and that your relationship with the Lord has grown because of it. He loves you so much and He'll continue to whisper as you continue to listen. He's such a great God!

Let's Connect!

www.mellieboozer.com

Facebook: Mellie Boozer- Author Page

Instagram: @mellieboozer

Email: hello@mellieboozer.com

I would love to hear how this book has encouraged or helped you. Feel free to inquire about my availability for speaking engagements at churches, organizations or events, as well.

One more thing! Please consider reviewing this devotional online at your purchase site. Leaving a review will help others learn about 'Whispers From God' and encourage them to experience this 30-day journey, too. Thank you!